WORKBOOK

For

It's Your Ship:

Leadership Strategies from the Best
Damn Ship in the Navy

Irene Franklin

Copyright © 2024 by Irene Franklin

All rights are reserved. Irene Franklin owns the intellectual property rights to this publication, including the content, photos, and other materials. Without the copyright holder's prior explicit agreement, no part of this book may be reproduced, distributed, or transmitted in any way, including photocopying, recording, or electronic techniques. Excerpts for critical evaluations and certain non-commercial purposes as authorized under copyright law are exempt.

This workbook functions as a supplementary educational aid, not a replacement for the original work. Its purpose is to facilitate comprehension and engagement with the primary content. The creator of this workbook is not associated with the copyright owner of the original publication, and any mention of it is purely for educational objectives.

Table of Contents

How to Use this Workbook 1

Overview 5

Chapter 1: Take Command 9

Chapter 2: Lead by Example 17

Chapter 3: Listen aggressively 25

Chapter 4: Communicate the purpose and meaning 31

Chapter 5: Create a Trusting Environment 37

CHAPTER 6: LOOK FOR RESULTS, NOT SALUTES 43

Chapter 7: Take Calculated Risks 51

Chapter 8: Go Beyond Standard Procedure 57

Chapter 9: Building Up Your People 65

Chapter 10: Generate Unity 73

Chapter 11: Improving Your People's Quality of Life 81

Chapter 12: Life After Benfold 89

Self-Evaluation Questions 97

HOW TO USE THIS WORKBOOK

Welcome to the companion workbook for Captain D. Michael Abrashoff's book, "It's Your Ship: Management Techniques from the Best Damn Ship in the Navy." This workbook is intended to provide a methodical strategy to engaging with the book's subject on a deeper level. It seeks to assist you in implementing successful leadership ideas by summarizing major chapters, emphasizing key insights, presenting self-reflection questions, giving life-changing exercises, and prompting self-evaluation.

This companion workbook is meant to support "It's Your Ship: Management Techniques from the Best Damn Ship in the Navy" by Captain D. Michael Abrashoff. It is not a replacement for the original work, but rather a tool for learning about and using its leadership ideas. Use this worksheet in combination with the text for a thorough comprehension.

Guidelines for using the workbook:

- Chapter Summaries: Each chapter summary summarizes the primary ideas and insights discussed in the corresponding chapter of "It's Your Ship." These summaries can be used as a refresher or a brief review of key points before beginning the workbook tasks.

- Main insights: After studying each chapter summary, make a note of the important insights that connect with you. These ideas serve as a foundation for further contemplation and use of the book's leadership approaches in your own workplace.

- Self-Reflection Questions: Following the chapter summaries, you will discover self-reflection questions meant to prompt further thought and analysis of how Abrashoff's concepts might be used in your leadership practice. Take your time with these questions and consider writing down your answers for clarity.

- Life-Changing Exercises: This workbook contains a variety of exercises inspired by the teachings from "It's Your Ship." These activities are designed to help you put the book's principles into practice while also encouraging personal and professional development. Choose workouts that you enjoy and commit to implementing them into your daily regimen for long-term results.

- Self-Evaluation Questions: At the end of the workbook, you'll discover self-evaluation questions to help you track your success and growth as you implement the book's leadership concepts. Use these questions to evaluate your accomplishments, identify areas for growth, and create goals for future development.

OVERVIEW

Captain D. Michael Abrashoff's book It's Your Ship: Management Techniques from the Best Damn Ship in the Navy is a captivating narrative of navy leadership and management, with principles that may be applied to any company or team. Abrashoff was given command of the USS Benfold, a ship known for inefficiency and low morale. He rebuilt the ship into one of the most successful in the Navy, establishing a reputation for operational efficiency and high crew satisfaction because to his distinct and inventive leadership style.

The basis of Abrashoff's leadership philosophy is the belief that leadership is about people, not processes or hierarchies. He emphasizes the value of trust, communication, and empowerment. He thinks that leaders should set an example for their teams, demonstrating that they are just as devoted to the purpose as everyone else. This method promotes mutual respect and encourages people to take ownership of their jobs and responsibilities.

One of the most important aspects of Abrashoff's approach was his willingness to listen. He discovered that the individuals closest to the task frequently had the best suggestions for improving procedures and getting better results. By aggressively seeking feedback from his workers, he was able to adopt adjustments that not only increased productivity but also morale. This method stands in stark contrast to typical top-down management systems, in which individuals at the top make choices with minimal input from those who are immediately affected by those decisions.

Abrashoff emphasizes the necessity of straightforward communication. He saw that in order for his team to be truly involved in their job, they needed to understand the "why" behind their assignments. By expressing purpose and meaning, he was able to coordinate the crew's activities with the ship's overall objective. This clarity of purpose also helped to reduce redundant duties and streamline processes, resulting in more effective and efficient performance.

Trust is another major element in It's Your Ship. Abrashoff worked hard to establish an environment in which his workers felt comfortable expressing their ideas, taking chances, and making errors. He understood that people perform best when they feel trusted and supported, not micromanaged or paralyzed by dread of failure. By creating a trusting environment, he was able to unleash his team's full potential.

Furthermore, Abrashoff's leadership style was distinguished by a readiness to deviate from convention when it was deemed appropriate. He questioned the established quo, fostered innovation, and took calculated risks. This willingness to think beyond the box was critical in making the USS Benfold an example of efficiency and success.

Abrashoff's It's Your Ship serves as a compelling reminder that effective leadership is about encouraging people to do their best, not about command and control. His narrative serves as an example to leaders in various industries, illustrating that with the appropriate attitude, even the most difficult conditions can be turned around to create an environment of greatness. The principles in this book are ageless, providing practical guidance that can be used by any business looking to increase performance, morale, and overall success.

CHAPTER 1: TAKE COMMAND

Chapter Summary:

In Chapter 1 of It's Your Ship, Captain D. Michael Abrashoff emphasizes the significance of taking charge of your tasks and crew. When he gained command of the USS Benfold, he discovered a dejected and disaffected crew, as well as an underperforming ship. Rather of just maintaining traditional naval authority, Abrashoff sought to set an example by altering the ship's culture. He understood that effective leadership necessitated personal accountability and a commitment to good change. Abrashoff made it his job to listen and comprehend his crew's worries. By doing so, he gained their respect and trust, which was critical to the turnaround. He stressed the necessity of clearly defining expectations, accepting responsibility for both triumphs and mistakes, and ensuring that everyone on the team feels appreciated and driven. Taking authority is not just issuing commands, but also accepting responsibility for the outcomes, whether favorable or poor.

Key takeaways:

- Leadership is about taking responsibility for outcomes.
- Listening to your team promotes trust and respect.
- Creating clear expectations is the first step in empowering people.
- Personal accountability is critical to good leadership.
- Change begins with you; model the conduct you anticipate.
- Understanding and resolving your team's problems can help increase engagement.
- Leading by example is more effective than leading by directives.
- Create a culture of mutual respect and a dedication to excellence.

Self-Reflective Questions:

Do you fully accept responsibility for the consequences of your actions?

_____

_____

_____

_____

_____

How effectively do you listen to your teammates' concerns?

_____

_____

_____

_____

_____

_____

_____

Do you have clear expectations for your team?

_____

_____

_____

_____

_____

_____

_____

_____

How do you model the conduct you hope to see in others?

_____

_____

_____

_____

_____

_____

_____

_____

Do you take proactive steps to handle issues, or do you react after the fact?

_____

_____

_____

_____

_____

How do you build a culture of respect and accountability among your team members?

_____

_____

_____

_____

_____

_____

Life-changing Exercises:

Reflect on a recent failure and determine what you could have done differently.

Schedule one-on-one sessions with your staff to better understand their concerns.

Make a list of specific expectations for your job and share it with your team.

Create a personal accountability strategy and commit to it.

Examine how you lead during a crisis and discover opportunities for growth.

Create a list of ways you can model the behavior you want your team to exhibit.

Hold a team meeting centered on mutual respect and trust-building.

Create an action plan for your team's top three issues.

Determine one area in which you can take greater responsibility and act on it.

Commit to one behavioral modification that will enhance your leadership style.

CHAPTER 2: LEAD BY EXAMPLE

Chapter Summary:

Chapter 2 focuses on the notion of leading by example. Captain Abrashoff exemplifies this by explaining how he modeled the habits and work ethic that he demanded from his men. He saw that people are more likely to follow a leader who demonstrates what they preach. Abrashoff established the tone by being accessible, personable, and fully engaged in the ship's daily operations. He was not afraid to undertake the grunt labor personally, which motivated his colleagues to follow suit. By setting a good example, he demonstrated to his crew that he was entirely devoted to the USS Benfold's success and expected them to be as well. This technique helps to break down rank boundaries while also instilling a sense of camaraderie and common purpose. Finally, leading by example entails maintaining integrity, consistency, and showing the behaviors and attitudes you wish to see in others.

Key takeaways:

- Leadership by example fosters a culture of honesty.
- When it comes to leadership, actions speak louder than words.
- Consistency in conduct fosters trust within your staff.
- Being active and visible promotes respect and accountability.
- Leading by example necessitates humility and a willingness to undertake the difficult job.
- Your team will reflect your devotion and effort.
- Integrity is critical; practice what you preach.
- A leader's example sets the tone for the team's actions.

Self-Reflective Questions:

Are your actions consistent with your words?

_____

_____

_____

_____

_____

_____

How visible and available are you to your teammates?

_____

_____

_____

_____

_____

_____

_____

Are you willing to work hard alongside your teammates?

_____
_____
_____
_____
_____
_____
_____

How constant are your behaviors and decisions?

_____
_____
_____
_____
_____
_____
_____

Do you demonstrate the degree of devotion that you demand from others?

_____

_____

_____

_____

_____

_____

_____

How can you display integrity as a leader?

_____

_____

_____

_____

_____

_____

Life-changing Exercises:

Identify one area where your behaviors may not be consistent with your statements and rectify it.

Make an effort to be more visible and accessible to your teammates.

Volunteer for a difficult duty that your team typically handles.

Commit to a daily routine that demonstrates the conduct you wish to see in others.

Consider how your behavior affects your team's behaviors and attitudes.

For one week, make sure your decisions and behaviors are consistent.

Observe how your team reacts to your leadership style and make adjustments as needed.

Take on a duty that is outside of your normal scope to set an example.

Discuss the value of integrity with your team and how to sustain it.

Set a personal aim of leading by example in all facets of your job.

CHAPTER 3: LISTEN AGGRESSIVELY

Chapter Summary:

In Chapter 3, Captain Abrashoff emphasizes the effectiveness of active listening as a leadership skill. He discovered that many leaders fail to properly listen to their teams, resulting in disengagement and wasted opportunities. Abrashoff made it a point to actively and attentively listen to his staff, knowing that people closest to the task frequently had the most valuable suggestions. By fostering an atmosphere in which his team felt heard and respected, he was able to unleash their creativity and problem-solving ability, resulting in unique ideas and enhanced performance. Listening aggressively entails being receptive to input, even if it is uncomfortable. Abrashoff recognized that listening involves more than simply hearing words; it also entails grasping the underlying concerns and motives. This technique allowed him to develop great relationships with his team and establish a culture of continual development.

Key takeaways:

Aggressive listening leads to useful insights from your team.

Being truly attentive fosters trust and rapport.

Listening actively promotes engagement and motivation.

Even if it is painful, feedback is essential for development.

Understanding the underlying problems of your team is critical for good leadership.

Creating an open culture promotes creativity and progress.

Listening is a very effective skill for developing good relationships.

True listening entails understanding and resolving issues.

Self-Reflective Questions:

How attentively do you listen to your team's problems and ideas?

_____

_____

_____

_____

_____

_____

Are you open to receiving critique, even if it is uncomfortable?

_____

_____

_____

_____

_____

_____

Do you aggressively seek feedback from people closest to the work?

_____

_____

_____

_____

_____

_____

How do you establish an environment in which your staff feels heard?

_____

_____

_____

_____

_____

_____

_____

Do you understand your team's core issues and motivations?

_____

_____

_____

_____

_____

_____

_____

How do you utilize listening to establish relationships?

_____

_____

_____

_____

_____

_____

_____

Life-changing Exercises:

Schedule time for one-on-one interactions with team members.

In your next meeting, practice active listening, with an emphasis on comprehending rather than responding.

Get input from your team and act on it.

Evaluate your listening skills and find areas for development.

Create a strategy to ensure that your staff feels heard and respected.

Encourage free discourse in meetings, allowing for everyone's input.

Keep a log of the insights you acquired while listening to your team.

Practice summarizing what you hear to ensure comprehension.

Implement one of your team's ideas and give them credit.

Regularly check in with your staff to assess their issues and motivations.

CHAPTER 4: COMMUNICATE THE PURPOSE AND MEANING.

Chapter Summary:

Chapter 4 emphasizes the necessity of expressing purpose and meaning to your team. Captain Abrashoff recognized that individuals work best when they understand the "why" of their duties. He made it a point to ensure that every crew member aboard the USS Benfold understood the importance of their job and how it related to the ship's broader goal. By connecting everyday chores to the greater goal, Abrashoff inspired his team to take pleasure in their job and strive for greatness. This strategy also helped to reduce needless activities and expedite operations because the staff knew what was most essential. Communicating purpose and meaning entails being open and honest with your team, which promotes trust and alignment. When employees appreciate the importance of their job, they are more likely to be motivated, engaged, and dedicated to meeting the team's objectives. Chapter Summary:

Key takeaways:

- People perform best when they understand the goal of their labor.
- Communicating the "why" instills pride and dedication.
- Linking tasks to the larger picture increases motivation.
- Transparency and honesty foster trust in a team.
- Purpose-driven work results in more simplified processes and efficiency.
- Understanding the relevance of work increases engagement.
- Aligning individual duties with general goals improves team effectiveness.
- Clear communication of intent is critical for attaining greatness.

Self-Reflective Questions:

Do you convey the aim of your team's tasks?

_____

_____

_____

_____

_____

_____

How successfully do you relate everyday work to the overall mission?

_____

_____

_____

_____

_____

_____

Are you open and honest in your communications?

_____

_____

_____

_____

_____

_____

How can you instill pride and devotion in your team?

_____

_____

_____

_____

_____

_____

_____

_____

Are your team's tasks in line with the overarching goals?

_____

_____

_____

_____

_____

_____

How can you make sure your staff realizes the relevance of their work?

_____

_____

_____

_____

_____

_____

Life-changing Exercises:

Spend time describing the "why" of a key activity or endeavor.

Consider how well you convey purpose to your team.

Determine where transparency may be enhanced and take action.

Create a visual picture of how each activity contributes to the broader purpose.

Hold a team meeting to discuss how to better connect daily duties with overall goals.

Practice connecting each job you give to its larger objective.

Investigate how knowing purpose affects your team's performance.

Encourage your staff to examine the "why" underlying their job.

Celebrate accomplishments that are consistent with the overall aim to reaffirm purpose.

Review and remove tasks that do not add to the overall goals.

CHAPTER 5: CREATE A TRUSTING ENVIRONMENT

Chapter Summary:

In Chapter 5, Captain Abrashoff highlights the significance of fostering a culture of trust among a team. He recognized that trust is the basis for effective leadership and high-performing teams. On the USS Benfold, Abrashoff strove to create an environment in which his crew felt comfortable expressing their ideas, taking chances, and even making errors without fear of repercussions. He understood that individuals work better when they feel trusted and supported. He was able to realize his crew's full potential by delegating authority and encouraging them to take ownership of their job. Trust also entails being dependable and consistent in your behaviors as a leader, so your team knows they can rely on you. Abrashoff's approach to developing trust was founded on mutual respect and genuine care for his crew's well-being, resulting in a more unified and successful team.

Key takeaways:

- Trust is the basis for good leadership.
- People perform better when they feel trusted and supported.
- Creating a safe workplace promotes creativity and risk-taking.
- Autonomy and ownership result in increased levels of involvement.
- Consistency and dependability foster confidence within a team.
- Mutual respect is essential for creating a trustworthy environment.
- Trust enables people to express themselves and take chances without fear.
- A culture of trust fosters a more cohesive and successful team.

Self-Reflective Questions:

How do you foster a culture of trust within your team?

_____

_____

_____

_____

_____

_____

Do your activities constantly foster trust among your team?

_____

_____

_____

_____

_____

_____

How do you promote autonomy and ownership?

_____

_____

_____

_____

_____

_____

_____

Are you a trustworthy and consistent leader?

_____

_____

_____

_____

_____

_____

_____

_____

_____

How can you encourage mutual respect in your team?

Do you provide a safe atmosphere for risk-taking and innovation?

Life-changing Exercises:

Consider how you develop or undermine trust in your leadership.

Identify one technique to give your team members additional liberty.

For one week, make sure your decisions and behaviors are consistent.

Hold a meeting aimed at increasing trust and mutual respect.

Encourage and encourage your team members when they take measured risks.

Observe how your team responds to autonomy and make any adjustments.

Set a personal goal to become more dependable and consistent in your leadership.

Make an action plan to resolve any trust concerns on your team.

Try being more honest and upfront with your team.

Concentrate on developing closer ties with your team members.

CHAPTER 6: LOOK FOR RESULTS, NOT SALUTES

Chapter Summary:

Chapter 6 discusses how good leaders should focus on results rather than seeking praise or reverence. Captain Abrashoff noticed that conventional military culture frequently promoted unquestioning obedience and saluting. However, he thought that genuine success is achieved by meaningful results rather than just following routine. On the USS Benfold, he urged his crew to focus on results and gave them the authority to determine the best means to achieve them. This strategy resulted in a more imaginative and results-oriented team. Abrashoff's emphasis on outcomes over salutes meant that he rewarded contributions based on their impact rather than the contributor's position. This egalitarian approach promoted a meritocratic society in which ideas were evaluated based on their merit rather than their origins. By emphasizing outcomes, Abrashoff was able to significantly increase the ship's performance and morale.

Key takeaways:

- Focus on creating significant results rather than simply following routine.
- Encourage creativity by giving your staff the freedom to develop the best solutions.
- Contributions are valued based on their effect rather than the contributor's rank.
- Prioritizing results produces a more productive and motivated team.
- A meritocratic culture encourages creativity and performance.
- Outcomes matter more than loyalty to conventional hierarchies.
- Emphasizes the need of focusing on results rather than just solutions.
- Effective leadership includes prioritizing genuine accomplishments over symbolic gestures.
- Focusing on results fosters a culture of continual growth and responsibility.

Self-Reflective Questions:

Are you more concerned about following process or producing actual results?

_____

_____

_____

_____

_____

_____

How do you encourage your team to come up with unique solutions?

_____

_____

_____

_____

_____

_____

Do you appreciate contributions based on their effect rather than their ranking?

_____

_____

_____

_____

_____

_____

_____

How do you assess success and effectiveness within your team?

_____

_____

_____

_____

_____

_____

_____

Are there any places where you may be choosing appearance over results?

_____

_____

_____

_____

_____

_____

How do you create a culture of merit and accountability?

_____

_____

_____

_____

_____

_____

Life-changing Exercises:

Identify a current project or assignment and assess it based on outcomes rather than processes.

Create a method to recognize and reward influence and innovation.

Review your method to evaluating team contributions and make changes to focus on outcomes.

Create criteria for measuring results and make sure they are followed consistently.

Encourage your team to suggest and try novel ways to achieve goals.

Consider how you might minimize the emphasis on protocol in favor of results-oriented initiatives.

Set up a feedback loop to evaluate the success of focusing on results.

Celebrate and emphasize accomplishments based on their significance, not their status or formality.

Hold a team meeting to discuss and agree on results-driven objectives.

Create an action plan to overcome any obstacles to attaining significant outcomes.

CHAPTER 7: TAKE CALCULATED RISKS

Chapter Summary:

Chapter 7 underscores the value of taking cautious risks in leadership. Captain Abrashoff recognized that innovation and growth frequently entail venturing outside of one's comfort zone and questioning the status quo. On the USS Benfold, he urged his crew to take risks and try innovative techniques to enhance performance. Abrashoff emphasized that taking risks does not imply recklessness; rather, it entails rigorous analysis and preparation to guarantee that the potential advantages outweigh the probable drawbacks. By creating an environment in which measured risks were welcomed and supported, he was able to achieve big changes and breakthroughs. This strategy contributed to the development of a culture of experimenting and learning, with mistakes viewed as chances for progress rather than setbacks. Abrashoff's leadership in this area illustrates how taking risks may result in significant dividends while also cultivating a dynamic and resilient workforce.

Key takeaways:

- Taking reasonable risks can lead to innovation and progress.
- Risks should be carefully assessed to balance possible rewards and drawbacks.
- Encouraging risk-taking develops an environment of exploration and learning.
- Failures should be viewed as chances for progress, not setbacks.
- Effective risk management requires both support and strategy.
- A culture that accepts risk can result in important discoveries.
- Effective leaders foster an environment in which measured risks are welcomed.
- Learning from risks and mistakes helps to ensure long-term success.

Self-Reflective Questions:

Are you open to taking calculated chances in your leadership role?

_____

_____

_____

_____

_____

How do you assess and plan for the potential risks and rewards?

_____

_____

_____

_____

_____

_____

Do you foster an environment in which your team is comfortable taking risks?

_____
_____
_____
_____
_____
_____
_____

How do you handle failures and setbacks caused by risks?

_____
_____
_____
_____
_____
_____
_____

Are you capable of distinguishing between reckless and measured risks?

How do you assist and encourage your team to take risks?

Life-changing Exercises:

Find a project where you can take a measured risk and devise a strategy for it.

Consider previous risks you've made and analyze their results.

Develop risk assessment criteria and apply them to a current situation.

Create a secure area for your team to propose and test new ideas.

Analyze a recent failure and determine the major lessons learnt.

Encourage your staff to discuss their experiences taking chances and the outcomes.

Set up a method to assess the effectiveness of risk-taking efforts.

Review your current risk tolerance and make any required adjustments.

Create a risk management plan for a forthcoming project.

Foster a resilient culture by talking about how to learn from setbacks.

CHAPTER 8: GO BEYOND STANDARD PROCEDURE

Chapter Summary:

In Chapter 8, Captain Abrashoff advises going above and beyond traditional processes to attain greatness. He argued that rigorously following old procedures frequently stifled creativity and efficiency. On the USS Benfold, Abrashoff urged his crew to think imaginatively and try new techniques to improve performance. He understood that, while procedures give a structure, they should not stifle innovation or limit the implementation of best practices. By questioning the status quo and pursuing improvements beyond routine processes, Abrashoff was able to make changes that resulted in increased efficiency and effectiveness. This strategy also entailed evaluating old processes and remaining open to new ideas from all levels of the business. Going beyond traditional methods necessitates a commitment to innovate and always seek new ways to attain goals.

Key takeaways:

- Standard processes can stifle creativity and efficiency.
- Encouraging innovative thinking can result in improved practices and outcomes.
- Challenging the status quo is critical to continual progress.
- Procedures should give a structure while not limiting creativity.
- Excellence is driven by a willingness to consider new ideas at all levels.
- Questioning old methods can result in major improvements.
- Creativity and innovation are essential for reaching improved performance.
- Going above and beyond normal practices develops an excellence-oriented culture.

Self-Reflective Questions:

Are you prepared to question established practices in order to discover better ways of doing things?

_____

_____

_____

_____

_____

How open are you to receiving fresh ideas and innovative thinking from your team?

_____

_____

_____

_____

_____

_____

Do you challenge established processes in order to make improvements?

How do you strike a balance between adherence to procedures and the desire for innovation?

Are you proactive in identifying and adopting best practices?

_____

_____

_____

_____

_____

_____

How can you create a culture that encourages employees to go above and beyond normal procedures?

_____

_____

_____

_____

_____

_____

_____

Life-changing Exercises:

Examine and assess current procedures to discover opportunities for improvement.

Encourage your staff to think and develop fresh approaches to achieve goals.

Implement a novel technique or strategy that challenges the established procedure.

Consider how prior breakthroughs have boosted your performance.

Create a strategy for consistently seeking and implementing best practices.

Create a feedback loop to evaluate the effectiveness of the modifications made.

Discuss with your team how to strike a balance between traditional processes and unique ideas.

Experiment with various methods to ordinary activities and assess the outcomes.

Identify a current problem and devise a novel solution that goes beyond typical practices.

Create an atmosphere in which questioning and improving procedures are encouraged.

CHAPTER 9: BUILDING UP YOUR PEOPLE

Chapter Summary:

Chapter 9 stresses the necessity of developing your people as a key component of good leadership. Captain Abrashoff realized that the USS Benfold's success was dependent on his crew's development and well-being. He prioritized his team's professional and personal development. This included creating opportunities for improvement, providing constructive comments, and celebrating accomplishments. Abrashoff recognized that when individuals feel appreciated and supported, they are more inclined to engage and perform at their peak. Building up your employees entails assisting them in developing their skills and capacities, which helps to the organization's overall success. Abrashoff's method fostered a pleasant and encouraging environment in which people were encouraged to maximize their potential, resulting in a more productive and cohesive team.

Key takeaways:

- Investing in your team's growth is critical to organizational success.
- Providing chances for growth allows people to attain their greatest potential.
- Constructive comments and praise are critical to developing your employees.
- Supporting your team, both personally and professionally, increases engagement.
- A good and encouraging atmosphere promotes greater performance.
- Helping team members improve their abilities leads to overall success.
- Valuing and supporting your team improves their cohesion and effectiveness.
- Developing your people results in a more motivated and capable workforce.

Self-Reflective Questions:

How do you support the development of your team members?

_____

_____

_____

_____

_____

Do you provide possibilities for your staff to advance professionally?

_____

_____

_____

_____

_____

_____

How do you provide constructive comments and celebrate achievements?

_____

_____

_____

_____

_____

_____

How do you provide personal and professional assistance to your team members?

_____

_____

_____

_____

_____

_____

How can you foster a pleasant and encouraging atmosphere for your team?

_____

_____

_____

_____

_____

_____

Are you assisting your team members in developing their skills and capabilities?

_____

_____

_____

_____

_____

_____

Life-changing Exercises:

Create and implement individual growth plans for each team member.

Schedule frequent one-on-one sessions to discuss your professional objectives and progress.

Create a mechanism to recognize and celebrate team accomplishments.

Provide constructive criticism and suggestions for improvement.

Create and provide training and mentorship opportunities for your workforce.

Consider how your assistance has influenced your team's performance and engagement.

Encourage team members to set personal and professional objectives, and help them achieve them.

Conduct a poll to obtain feedback on how well you assist and grow your staff.

Make a strategy to address any skill or development gaps on your staff.

Develop a culture of constant learning and progress.

CHAPTER 10: GENERATE UNITY

Chapter Summary:

Chapter 10 examines the importance of fostering team cohesiveness. Captain Abrashoff recognized the benefits of a united team, including increased effectiveness and resilience. On the USS Benfold, he strove to instill a feeling of common purpose and togetherness in his crew. This included building solid relationships, encouraging teamwork, and instilling a sense of communal responsibility. Abrashoff felt that unity is achieved by recognizing and respecting each other's contributions, as well as working toward similar goals. He was able to improve the links amongst his crew members by facilitating team-building activities and open communication. Creating unity also entails resolving problems constructively and making sure that every team member feels included and respected. A cohesive team is more motivated, engaged, and capable of meeting its goals.

Key takeaways:

- Unity within a team improves effectiveness and resilience.
- Developing a common sense of purpose encourages friendship and teamwork.
- Strong relationships and open communication are critical to achieving unity.
- Valuing one another's efforts fosters a shared feeling of responsibility.
- Team-building exercises boost relationships and improve teamwork.
- Constructive dispute resolution adds to a cohesive team.
- Inclusion and acknowledgment make all team members feel valued.
- A cohesive team is more motivated and capable of accomplishing objectives.

Self-Reflective Questions:

How do you build a feeling of togetherness and shared purpose among your team members?

_____

_____

_____

_____

_____

_____

What efforts do you take to foster connections and collaboration?

_____

_____

_____

_____

_____

How do you approach disagreements such that they may be resolved constructively?

Are you generating possibilities for teamwork and open communication?

How do you make sure every team member feels included and valued?

_____

_____

_____

_____

_____

_____

What tactics do you employ to foster a common sense of responsibility?

_____

_____

_____

_____

_____

_____

Life-changing Exercises:

Plan a team-building event to improve connections and collaboration.

Create and execute techniques for dealing with and resolving disputes constructively.

Create a strategy for improving open communication and ensuring that all voices are heard.

Consider how your behaviors help or impede team cohesiveness.

Encourage team members to openly discuss their thoughts and viewpoints.

Set up frequent check-ins to review team chemistry and resolve any difficulties.

Celebrate team accomplishments and individual efforts to build a feeling of community.

Create a team charter articulating common aims and values to strengthen togetherness.

Implement feedback methods to better understand and meet team members' needs for inclusion.

Create chances for team members to work together on projects and responsibilities.

CHAPTER 11: IMPROVING YOUR PEOPLE'S QUALITY OF LIFE

Chapter Summary:

Chapter 11 emphasizes the necessity of increasing your team's quality of life. Captain Abrashoff observed that a friendly and caring work atmosphere improves overall job satisfaction and performance. On the USS Benfold, he prioritized ensuring that his crew had access to resources, support, and chances to improve their well-being. This entailed meeting both professional and personal demands, such as creating a healthy work atmosphere, encouraging work-life balance, and fostering individual growth. Abrashoff recognized that when individuals feel cared for and respected, they are more inclined to engage and perform at their peak. Improving your employees' quality of life entails being attentive to their needs and establishing an atmosphere in which they may succeed professionally and personally.

Key takeaways:

- Improving the quality of life for your staff leads to higher work satisfaction and performance.
- Addressing both professional and personal demands promotes total well-being.
- A pleasant work environment and work-life balance are essential for engagement.
- Individual growth fosters a sense of worth and fulfillment.
- Being aware of your team's needs promotes a caring and supportive atmosphere.
- Providing resources and opportunity for advancement improves the quality of life.
- A emphasis on well-being improves performance and work happiness.
- Creating an atmosphere in which individuals can thrive helps teams succeed.

Self-Reflective Questions:

How do you meet your team's professional and personal needs?

_____

_____

_____

_____

_____

_____

What efforts do you take to foster a healthy working environment?

_____

_____

_____

_____

_____

_____

_____

How do you foster work-life balance among your team members?

_____

_____

_____

_____

_____

_____

What methods do you encourage personal development and growth?

_____

_____

_____

_____

_____

_____

Are you responsive to your team's needs and concerns?

_____
_____
_____
_____
_____
_____

How can you make sure that your team members feel appreciated and cared for?

_____
_____
_____
_____
_____
_____

Life-changing Exercises:

Develop and implement programs to help your staff achieve better work-life balance.

Conduct a poll to obtain feedback on how successfully you meet your team's requirements.

Create a strategy to improve the workplace and support your team's well-being.

Provide resources and opportunity for both personal and professional growth.

Consider how enhancing quality of life affects your team's performance and happiness.

Set up frequent check-ins to discuss and resolve individual needs and problems.

Encourage open discussion about well-being and support among teammates.

Create programs or events that will boost team morale and involvement.

Review and modify policies to improve work-life balance and general quality of life.

Recognize and address the needs of team members to foster a caring and supportive workplace.

CHAPTER 12: LIFE AFTER BENFOLD

Chapter Summary:

Chapter 12 discusses life after Captain Abrashoff's time on the USS Benfold. Abrashoff explains how the beliefs and practices he embraced had a long-term influence on his leadership style and personal development. He provides insights on his ongoing path of applying what he learnt aboard the ship to new difficulties and possibilities. Abrashoff emphasizes that leadership is an ongoing process of learning and adjusting. Life after Benfold entailed carrying on the ideals and practices that contributed to the ship's success while also welcoming fresh viewpoints and chances for progress. Abrashoff's experiences emphasize the significance of reflection and adaptation in leadership, indicating that good leadership ideas may be implemented and enhanced over a career.

Key takeaways:

- Leadership is an ongoing process of learning and adapting.

- The concepts implemented aboard the USS Benfold had a long-term influence on Abrashoff's leadership style.
- Reflecting on previous experiences assists in applying lessons to current situations.
- Embracing new viewpoints and possibilities promotes personal and professional development.
- Maintaining good techniques helps to ensure long-term success.
- Leadership concepts may be improved and applied throughout a person's career.
- Leadership development requires continuous learning and progress.
- Applying best practices from previous experiences can lead to future success.

Self-Reflective Questions:

How do you continue to learn and grow as a leader?

_____

_____

_____

_____

_____

What lessons from previous experiences have shaped your leadership style?

_____

_____

_____

_____

_____

_____

How do you reflect on and apply your learnings to new challenges?

_____

_____

_____

_____

_____

_____

_____

Are you open to new ideas and possibilities for growth?

_____

_____

_____

_____

_____

_____

_____

How do you continue effective methods from earlier experiences?

_____

_____

_____

_____

_____

What efforts do you take to continually enhance and polish your leadership style?

_____

_____

_____

_____

_____

_____

Life-changing Exercises:

Consider the essential lessons you've learnt from your previous leadership experiences.

Create a strategy for adapting successful methods to new difficulties.

Set personal and professional development objectives based on previous experiences.

Seek input from peers and mentors to obtain new insights on your leadership.

Review and modify your leadership style to include lessons learnt.

Create a notebook to keep track of your continuing leadership development and growth.

Identify places where you may seize fresh chances for development and progress.

Create a plan for continual learning and implementing good techniques.

Consider how your leadership values have grown and how they might continue to expand.

Share your experiences and lessons learnt with others to help them progress.

SELF-EVALUATION QUESTIONS

How can I successfully take authority and lead in difficult situations?

How do I lead by example, and how does this impact my team?

How well do I actively listen to my teammates, and how does this affect our communication?

Do I effectively explain the purpose and significance of assignments and goals to my team?

How can I foster and sustain a culture of trust within my team?

Am I concentrating on outcomes and performance rather than merely following normal processes and expectations?

How comfortable am I with taking calculated risks, and how do I manage and limit the potential consequences?

_____
_____
_____
_____
_____
_____
_____

How do I inspire and assist my team to think outside the box and innovate?

_____
_____
_____
_____
_____
_____
_____

How can I encourage and promote the professional and personal development of my team members?

_____

_____

_____

_____

_____

_____

What tactics do I employ to promote unity and a feeling of shared purpose in my team?

_____

_____

_____

_____

_____

_____

_____

How can I increase my team members' quality of life and overall job satisfaction?

_____

_____

_____

_____

_____

_____

How can I ensure that my leadership concepts and practices have a long-term good impact?

_____

_____

_____

_____

_____

_____

_____

How can I reflect on and apply lessons from previous experiences to present challenges?

_____

_____

_____

_____

_____

_____

What steps do I take to adjust and improve my leadership style in response to criticism and fresh perspectives?

_____

_____

_____

_____

_____

_____

How do I strike a balance between adhering to established protocols and allowing for innovation and improvement?

Made in United States
Troutdale, OR
03/03/2025